99

THINGS
THAT
BRING
ME JOY

by

ABRAMS NOTERIE, NEW YORK

· 1 ·

Childhood toys you loved

_____

_____

_____

_____

_____

_____

_____

_____

_____

_____

2

A beloved childhood film

3

Childhood books you treasure

4

Games you loved to play as a kid

5

*Childhood activities you
don't want to outgrow*

6 | *One memorable family vacation*

7 | *Your closest relatives*

8 | *Your oldest friend*

9 | *Your favorite holiday tradition*

10 | *A thoughtful gift you've received*

11 | *A gift you enjoyed giving to someone else*

12

One singularly
unforgettable
day in your life

13

Your best birthday celebrations

_____

_____

_____

_____

_____

_____

_____

_____

_____

_____

· 14 ·

Things you collect

15 | *A possession that has sentimental value*

16

A list of your favorite words

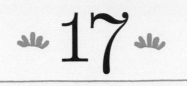

17

Your favorite color combinations

_____

_____

_____

_____

_____

_____

_____

_____

_____

_____

_____

18 | *A combination of flavors you love*

19 | *Your all-time favorite meal*

20

Your go-to snacks

_____

_____

_____

_____

_____

_____

_____

_____

_____

_____

_____

21 | *A devoted pet (or your favorite animals)*

22

Things you think are cute

23

Your favorite places in the world

_____

_____

_____

_____

_____

_____

_____

_____

_____

_____

_____

_____

24

Destinations you
dream of visiting

× 25 ×

Your best traveling companions

_____

_____

_____

_____

_____

_____

_____

_____

_____

26 | *A familiar sight that makes you feel grounded*

27 | *Your home away from home*

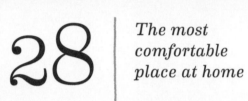

28 | The most comfortable place at home

29

The most useful things you own

30

The most beautiful things you own

31 | *A fulfilling household chore*

32 | *A task you love to finish*

33 | *Something you're looking forward to right now*

34 | A daily ritual you relish

35 | *Something you enjoy doing by yourself*

36 | *Something you never get tired of*

37 | A sensation you enjoy

38

*Little things that
make your day better*

_____

_____

_____

_____

_____

_____

_____

_____

_____

_____

39

One small
thing you'd like
to remember
about today

40

Things that make you feel healthy

41

A small way to
treat yourself

42 | *A compliment you've received*

43

A story that always makes you laugh

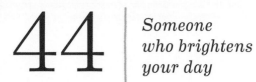

44 | *Someone who brightens your day*

45 | *A little victory*

46

A happy accident

47 | *An act of kindness you received*

48 | *An act of kindness you performed*

49

Movies you watch again and again

50

*Television shows
that help you escape*

51

Your favorite books

_____

_____

_____

_____

_____

_____

_____

_____

_____

_____

52 | *A colorful
character in
your life*

53

A fictional
character you
would love to
have as a friend

54 | *A work of art that inspires you*

55

A *favorite line from a book, movie, or television show*

56

Music you love

_____

_____

_____

_____

_____

_____

_____

_____

_____

_____

_____

57

Your favorite sounds

58

Your favorite scents

59 | *An aspect of nature that inspires you*

60

*Your favorite
outdoor activity*

61 | *Your favorite type of weather*

62 | *Your favorite season*

63 | *A subject that intrigues you right now*

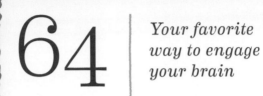

64 | *Your favorite way to engage your brain*

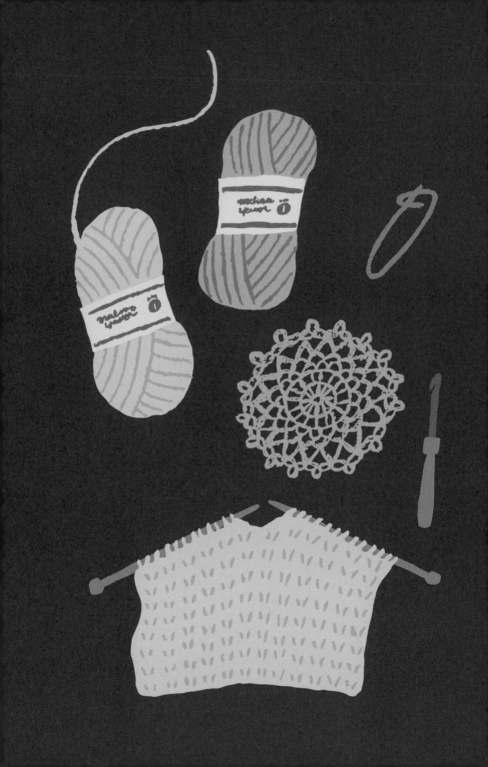

65

Things you can make
with your hands

66

Your secret talents

_____

_____

_____

_____

_____

_____

_____

_____

_____

_____

_____

67

Your not-so-secret talents

_____

_____

_____

_____

_____

_____

_____

_____

_____

_____

_____

68

Something you didn't expect to like, but did

69 | *A fantastic first*

70

Things that give you butterflies

71

Activities you find soothing

_____

_____

_____

_____

_____

_____

_____

_____

_____

_____

72

Your guilty pleasures

_____

_____

_____

_____

_____

_____

_____

_____

_____

_____

73 | The perfect way to play hooky for the day

74 | *Your own secret retreat*

75 | *An ideal weekend morning*

76 | *Your beverage of choice in the morning*

77

Your beverage
of choice in
the evening

78 | *Your favorite way to unwind at the end of the day*

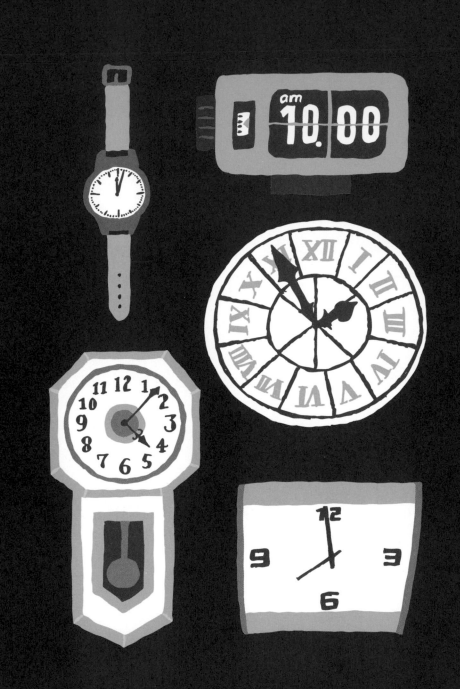

79

The time of
day when you're
at your best

80

The outfit that gives you a boost of confidence

81

Your comfiest clothes

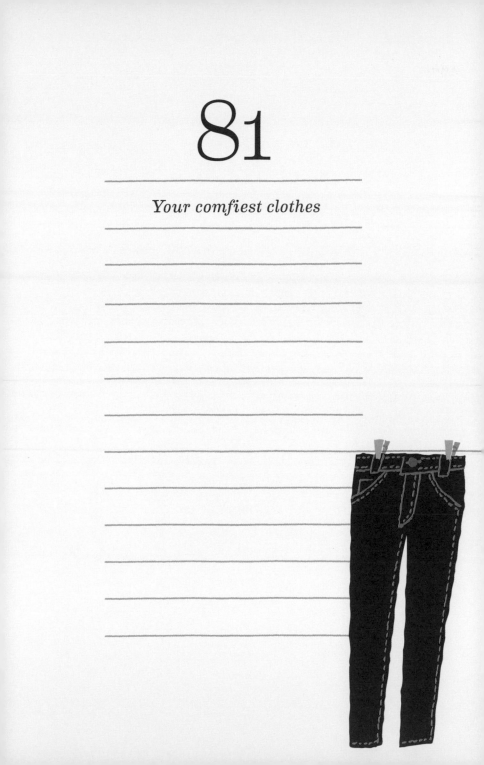

··· 82 ···

Clothing that feels the most "you"

83

Your best features

_____

_____

_____

_____

_____

_____

_____

_____

_____

_____

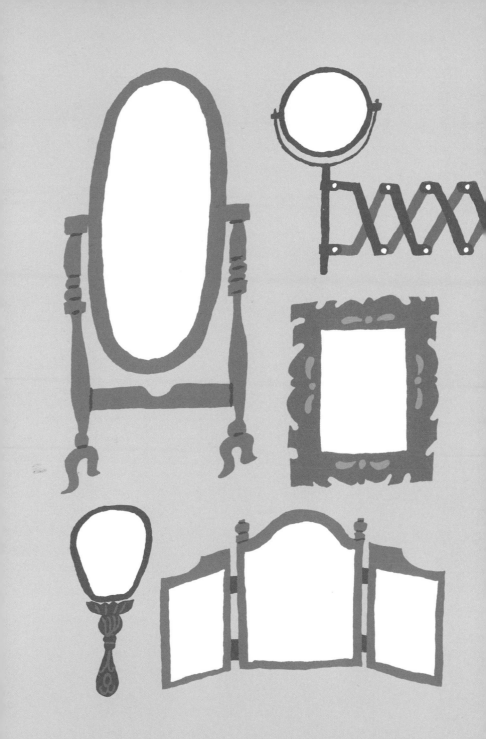

84 | Someone who gives you confidence

85 | *Someone who makes you laugh*

86 | Someone you admire

87 | An encouraging quote

88 | An accomplishment you're proud of

89 | *A struggle that paid off*

90 | *A community that gives you a sense of belonging*

91 | *Someone who has mentored you*

92 | *Someone you have mentored*

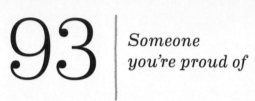

93 | *Someone you're proud of*

94 | *Someone you can always count on*

BEST FRIENDS

95

*The people you would
move mountains for*

_____

_____

_____

_____

_____

_____

_____

_____

_____

_____

96 | *A piece of wisdom someone gave you*

97

Something you've learned about yourself

_____

_____

_____

_____

_____

_____

_____

_____

_____

98 | *Your own strengths of character*